UNMASKING

THE ILLUSION

.

Debunking the Deepest Money Myths

By

Mjaafar Shaffah

Copyright Copy

Table of Contents

Introduction: Challenging the Status Quo

Money, wealth, and financial success are topics that captivate the human imagination. They are often seen as the markers of success, happiness, and security in our society. However, the pursuit of money and the accumulation of wealth are often shrouded in misconceptions, myths, and societal norms that can hinder our ability to achieve true financial success. In this book, we will challenge the status quo and delve deep into the deepest money myths that hold many people back from building wealth and achieving their financial goals.

Throughout history, there have been many widely accepted money myths that have shaped our perceptions and behaviors around money. These myths are often passed down from generation to generation, ingrained in our cultural beliefs, and reinforced by societal norms. They can create limiting beliefs, self-sabotaging behaviors, and financial struggles that prevent us from achieving financial success. It's time to challenge these myths and debunk them once and for all.

This book is not just about financial advice or money management tips. It goes beyond the typical "how-to" approach and delves into the psychological, emotional, and societal aspects of money. We will explore the underlying beliefs, attitudes, and behaviors that influence our financial decisions and outcomes. We will uncover the hidden money scripts that shape our thoughts and feelings about money. We will demystify the misconceptions that surround debt, consumerism, quick riches, social comparison, and other prevalent money myths. And most importantly, we will provide practical tools, insights, and strategies to help you rewrite your money story and achieve financial clarity and empowerment.

The world of money and wealth can be complex and challenging to navigate. It's easy to get caught up in the societal norms, financial pressures, and cultural expectations that dictate how we should handle our money. However, true financial success requires us to question and challenge the status quo. It requires us to critically examine our beliefs, attitudes, and behaviors around money and make conscious choices that align with our values, goals, and aspirations.

In this book, we will challenge the notion that money is the root of all evil, debunk the fallacy of get-rich-quick schemes, demystify the truth about debt, expose the illusion of consumerism, and demolish the myth of overnight success. We will also explore the impact of social comparison and societal expectations on our financial well-being and provide practical strategies to overcome these challenges.

Through thought-provoking exercises, real-life examples, and practical tips, this book will empower you to take control of your financial future, break free from the limitations of money myths, and embrace a new mindset that aligns with your true financial potential. Whether you're just starting your financial journey, struggling with debt, striving for financial independence, or looking to build wealth for future generations, this book will challenge your existing beliefs, provide new insights, and equip you with the tools to create lasting financial success.

It's time to challenge the status quo and break free from the misconceptions that hold you back from achieving your financial goals. It's time to demystify the deepest money myths and embark on a journey towards financial clarity and empowerment. Are you ready to challenge the status quo and transform your relationship with money? If so, let's dive in and uncover the truth about money, wealth, and financial success. Get ready to rewrite your money story and unlock your true financial potential!

Chapter 1: Money Mindset Matters: Understanding Your Relationship with Wealth

Money is more than just currency; it carries significant emotional, psychological, and societal weight. Our beliefs and attitudes about money, also known as our money mindset, play a crucial role in shaping our financial behavior and outcomes. In this chapter, we will explore the myths surrounding money and debunk the misconceptions that often hinder our ability to build wealth and achieve financial success.

Dispelling the Myth of Money as the Root of All Evil

Many of us have grown up with the belief that money is the root of all evil. We have been taught that those who pursue wealth are greedy, selfish, and morally corrupt. This deeply ingrained societal myth can create a negative association with money and hinder our ability to accumulate wealth. However, the truth is that money is simply a tool that can be used for both good and bad purposes. It is not money itself, but rather how we use it that determines its impact. Money has the power to create positive change, support our goals and dreams, and make a difference in our lives and the lives of others.

Examining Your Beliefs and Attitudes about Money

Our beliefs and attitudes about money are often shaped by our upbringing, cultural influences, and personal experiences. These beliefs can greatly impact our financial decision-making, habits, and overall financial well-being. In this chapter, we will delve deep into our own beliefs and attitudes about money and examine how they have influenced our financial behaviors. We will explore questions such as:

- What were you taught about money growing up?
- How do you perceive wealthy people?
- What emotions or thoughts arise when you think about money?
- Do you believe that money is scarce or abundant?
- What are your financial goals and aspirations?

Uncovering Hidden Money Scripts and Their Impact on Your Financial Life

Our beliefs and attitudes about money often manifest as internal scripts or narratives that shape our thoughts, feelings, and behaviors around money. These money scripts can be either empowering or limiting, and they can greatly impact our financial decisions and outcomes. In this chapter, we will uncover hidden money scripts that may be holding us back from achieving our financial goals. We will explore common money scripts such as:

- "Money is hard to come by."
- "I'm not good with money."
- "I'll never be wealthy, so why bother trying?"
- "Money is meant to be spent, not saved."
- "I need to rely on others to take care of my finances."

We will delve into the origins of these money scripts, their impact on our financial behaviors, and how we can rewrite them to create a more positive and empowering money mindset.

By the end of this chapter, you will have gained a deeper understanding of your relationship with money and the impact of your money mindset on your financial decisions and outcomes. You will be equipped with tools and insights to challenge and transform any limiting beliefs or attitudes about money that may be hindering your ability to build wealth and achieve financial success. Remember, your money mindset matters, and it's never too late to rewrite your money story for a brighter financial future.

Chapter 2: Money is Not the Root of All Evil

One of the most pervasive money myths that has been ingrained in our culture is the belief that money is the root of all evil. This notion has been passed down through generations, perpetuated by societal norms, and reinforced by religious teachings. Many people have been raised with the belief that money is inherently bad, that those who pursue wealth are selfish or greedy, and that accumulating wealth is morally wrong.

However, this belief is a distortion of the original biblical quote from 1 Timothy 6:10, which states, "For the love of money is a root of all kinds of evil." Notice that it is not money itself that is labeled as evil, but rather the unhealthy attachment and love for money that can lead to detrimental consequences. Money is simply a tool that can be used for both positive and negative purposes, depending on how it is acquired and used.

In fact, money can be a force for good. It can be used to create opportunities, support charitable causes, provide for our families, and make a positive impact on the world. Money can empower us to pursue our passions, invest in education and personal growth, and contribute to our communities. It is not inherently evil, but rather a neutral resource that can be used in various ways.

This money myth can have detrimental effects on our financial mindset and behaviors. If we believe that money is evil, we may unconsciously self-sabotage our financial success. We may feel guilty about wanting to accumulate wealth or pursue financial goals. We may shy away from opportunities to earn more money or invest in our financial education. We may feel conflicted about using money for personal enjoyment or fulfillment. These beliefs can create a negative mindset around money and hinder our ability to build wealth and achieve financial success.

It's time to challenge this money myth and shift our mindset towards a healthier relationship with money. Money is not inherently evil or good; it is simply a tool that can be used in different ways. It's our beliefs, attitudes, and behaviors around money that determine whether it has a positive or negative impact on our lives and the lives of those around us.

To overcome this money myth, it's important to reflect on our beliefs about money and question their validity. We need to examine the underlying reasons why we may hold negative beliefs about money, such as societal norms, religious teachings, or past experiences. We need to challenge these beliefs and replace them with a more balanced and empowering perspective on money.

It's also important to cultivate a healthy relationship with money by developing financial literacy, setting clear financial goals, and creating a plan to achieve them. We need to learn how to manage money wisely, invest strategically, and make conscious choices about how we use our resources. By developing a positive mindset towards money and embracing a responsible approach to managing our finances, we can overcome the belief that money is the root of all evil and instead use it as a powerful tool for creating the life we desire.

In conclusion, the belief that money is the root of all evil is a pervasive money myth that can hinder our ability to achieve financial success. Money is not inherently evil or good; it is a neutral resource that can be used in various ways. By challenging this myth and developing a healthy relationship with money, we can shift our mindset towards a more empowered and responsible approach to managing our finances. It's time to debunk this myth and embrace a new perspective on money that aligns with our financial goals and aspirations.

Chapter 3: Demystifying the Wealth Mindset

The way we think about wealth and success has a profound impact on our ability to achieve financial prosperity. Our mindset, or our set of attitudes and beliefs, shapes our financial behaviors and decisions. In this chapter, we will demystify the wealth mindset and explore how it can influence our financial outcomes.

One common money myth that can hinder our wealth mindset is the belief that wealth is reserved for the lucky few or the "chosen" ones. Many people may believe that they are not meant to be wealthy, that they do not have the skills, knowledge, or opportunities to accumulate wealth. This belief can create a sense of resignation and limit our financial aspirations and efforts.

However, the truth is that wealth is not solely determined by luck or fate. It is a result of conscious choices, strategic planning, and disciplined actions. Anyone, regardless of their background or circumstances, has the potential to build wealth with the right mindset and financial strategies in place.

In order to cultivate a wealth mindset, we need to shift our beliefs about wealth and success. We need to let go of limiting beliefs and replace them with empowering ones. We need to believe that we are capable of achieving financial success, that we deserve to be wealthy, and that there are ample opportunities for us to create wealth in our lives.

We also need to change our perception of wealth from being selfish or greedy to being a positive force for good. Wealth can enable us to create a better life for ourselves and our loved ones, contribute to our communities, and make a positive impact on the world. When we see wealth as a tool for creating positive change, we are more likely to pursue it with a sense of purpose and meaning.

Another important aspect of the wealth mindset is adopting a proactive and strategic approach to our finances. This includes setting clear financial goals, creating a budget and financial plan, and consistently taking actions that align with our financial objectives. It also involves developing financial literacy and continually educating ourselves about money management, investing, and wealth-building strategies. When we take charge of our financial future and actively work towards our goals, we are more likely to achieve them.

Moreover, a wealth mindset involves developing a positive relationship with money. We need to view money as a resource that can be managed wisely, invested strategically, and used to create opportunities and fulfill our financial goals. We need to overcome any fear or aversion towards money and instead embrace it as a tool that can support our financial well-being and enable us to live the life we desire.

In conclusion, cultivating a wealth mindset is essential for achieving financial success. It involves shifting our beliefs about wealth and success, seeing wealth as a positive force for good, adopting a proactive and strategic approach to our finances, and developing a healthy relationship with money. By demystifying the wealth mindset and adopting empowering beliefs and behaviors, we can overcome limitations, achieve our financial goals, and create a prosperous future for ourselves and our families.

Chapter 4: Debunking Common Money Myths

Our understanding of money is often shaped by common money myths that can impact our financial decisions and behaviors. In this chapter, we will debunk some of the most pervasive money myths that may be holding us back from achieving financial success.

Myth 1: "Money is the root of all evil"

This is a common misquote of a biblical verse that actually says, "For the love of money is a root of all kinds of evil" (1 Timothy 6:10). The key distinction here is that it is not money itself that is evil, but the excessive attachment or obsession with money that can lead to negative consequences. Money is simply a tool that can be used for good or bad purposes, depending on how it is managed and utilized.

Debunking this myth involves shifting our mindset from viewing money as inherently evil to seeing it as a neutral resource that can be used for positive purposes, such as providing for our needs, supporting our goals, and making a difference in the lives of others.

Myth 2: "You need to be rich to invest or build wealth"

This myth can discourage many people from even attempting to invest or build wealth, as they may believe that significant wealth is a prerequisite for such endeavors. However, this is not true. In fact, investing and building wealth can start with small steps, such as saving and investing in low-cost index funds, diversifying investments, and taking advantage of compound interest over time.

Debunking this myth involves recognizing that anyone, regardless of their current financial situation, can start investing and building wealth by taking small, consistent steps over time. It's not about the amount of money you start with, but rather the consistency and discipline of your savings and investment habits.

Myth 3: "Debt is always bad"

While it is true that excessive debt and high-interest rates can be detrimental to our financial well-being, not all debt is bad. In fact, strategically used debt, such as mortgages or student loans, can be leveraged to acquire assets or investments that can appreciate in value and generate wealth over time.

Debunking this myth involves understanding the difference between good debt and bad debt, and making informed decisions about when and how to use debt to our advantage. It's important to manage debt responsibly, pay attention to interest rates and terms, and have a plan in place to pay off debt strategically.

Myth 4: "Investing is too risky"

Many people may shy away from investing due to the perception of it being risky or complicated. However, not investing can also carry risks, such as inflation eroding the purchasing power of our money over time or missing out on potential returns from investment opportunities.

Debunking this myth involves gaining a basic understanding of investing principles, diversifying investments, and developing a long-term investment strategy that aligns with our financial goals and risk tolerance. It's important to approach investing with knowledge, research, and a balanced approach to manage risks effectively.

Myth 5: "You need a high income to become wealthy"

While a high income can certainly accelerate the wealth-building process, it is not the sole determinant of wealth. Many individuals with modest incomes have achieved significant wealth through careful budgeting, saving, and strategic investing.

Debunking this myth involves understanding that wealth is not solely determined by income, but rather by our ability to manage money effectively, live within our means, and make smart financial choices. It's about prioritizing savings and investments, and consistently working towards our financial goals, regardless of our income level.

In conclusion, debunking common money myths is crucial for developing a healthy and informed perspective on money and wealth. By challenging these myths and gaining a clear understanding of the realities of money management

Chapter 5: Building a Strong Financial Foundation

In order to achieve financial success and debunk money myths, it's important to establish a strong financial foundation. In this chapter, we will explore key principles and practices that can help us build a solid financial foundation and set ourselves up for long-term financial success.

Budgeting and Spending

Creating a budget is a fundamental step in managing our money effectively. It allows us to track our income, expenses, and savings, and ensures that our money is allocated wisely according to our priorities and goals. A budget helps us understand our spending patterns, identify areas where we can cut back or save more, and make informed decisions about our spending.

Debunking the myth that budgeting is restrictive or complicated involves understanding that budgeting is empowering and puts us in control of our money.

It helps us make intentional choices about how we want to use our money, and align our spending with our values and financial goals.

Saving and Emergency Fund

Saving money is a crucial component of building a strong financial foundation. It allows us to create a safety net for emergencies, unexpected expenses, or future goals. One common myth is that saving is only for the wealthy, but in reality, everyone can save regardless of their income level.

Debunking this myth involves recognizing the importance of saving and making it a priority in our financial plan. This includes setting up an emergency fund with three to six months of living expenses, automating our savings, and consistently saving a percentage of our income, no matter how small.

Debt Management

As discussed in the previous chapter, not all debt is bad, but it's important to manage it responsibly.

This includes paying off high-interest debt as soon as possible, avoiding unnecessary debt, and not relying on debt to finance a lifestyle beyond our means.

Debunking the myth that debt is unavoidable involves understanding that debt can be managed effectively with responsible borrowing and repayment strategies. This includes creating a debt repayment plan, negotiating lower interest rates, and seeking financial advice if needed.

Investing and Wealth Building

Investing is a key strategy for building wealth over the long term. Many people may feel intimidated or overwhelmed by the concept of investing, but with proper knowledge and guidance, it can be a powerful tool for growing our wealth.

Debunking the myth that investing is only for experts or the wealthy involves understanding that investing is for everyone, and it's never too early or too late to start. This includes gaining basic knowledge about different investment options, diversifying investments, and working with a qualified financial professional if needed.

Financial Education and Continuous Learning

Financial literacy is an essential aspect of building a strong financial foundation. It's important to continuously educate ourselves about personal finance, investment strategies, and best practices for managing money effectively.

Debunking the myth that financial education is only for experts involves recognizing that financial literacy is a lifelong journey. This includes reading books, attending workshops, listening to podcasts, and seeking advice from reputable sources to continuously improve our financial knowledge and decision-making skills.

In conclusion, building a strong financial foundation involves budgeting and spending wisely, saving and creating an emergency fund, managing debt responsibly, investing strategically, and continuously educating ourselves about personal finance. By following these principles and practices, we can debunk money myths and set ourselves up for long-term financial success.

Chapter 6: Overcoming Psychological Barriers to Financial Success

In addition to the practical strategies discussed in previous chapters, our mindset and beliefs about money play a crucial role in our financial success. In this chapter, we will explore common psychological barriers that can hinder our financial progress and learn how to overcome them.

Money Mindset

Our mindset and beliefs about money can shape our financial behaviors and outcomes. Many people hold negative or limiting beliefs about money, such as "money is evil," "I'm not good with money," or "I'll never be wealthy." These beliefs can create self-sabotaging behaviors, such as overspending, avoiding financial decisions, or not pursuing opportunities for wealth creation.

Debunking the myth that money is evil or that we are not capable of managing it involves shifting our mindset to a positive and empowering perspective. This includes cultivating a growth mindset, reframing our beliefs about money, and developing a healthy relationship with money based on gratitude, abundance, and empowerment.

Emotional Spending

Emotional spending is a common psychological barrier to financial success. Many people use spending as a way to cope with stress, emotions, or boredom. Emotional spending can lead to impulsive purchases, overspending, and accumulating debt.

Debunking the myth that material possessions can fill emotional voids involves developing healthy coping mechanisms for dealing with emotions, such as mindfulness, exercise, or talking to a trusted friend or therapist. It also involves being aware of our emotional triggers for spending and finding alternative ways to address those emotions without relying on spending.

Fear of Failure or Success

Fear of failure or success can also hinder our financial success. Fear of failure can prevent us from taking risks or pursuing opportunities for wealth creation, while fear of success can lead to self-sabotage or feelings of guilt or unworthiness.

Debunking the myth that failure or success defines our self-worth involves understanding that failure is a natural part of the learning process and success is achievable with hard work and perseverance. It also involves addressing any underlying fears or limiting beliefs about failure or success through self-reflection, self-compassion, and taking calculated risks.

Procrastination and Decision Paralysis

Procrastination and decision paralysis can prevent us from making timely and informed financial decisions. Many people may delay important financial tasks, such as budgeting, investing, or debt management, due to overwhelm, indecisiveness, or lack of confidence.

Debunking the myth that financial decisions are complicated or overwhelming involves breaking tasks into smaller, manageable steps, seeking help or advice when needed, and taking action despite uncertainty. It also involves developing decision-making skills, setting deadlines, and holding ourselves accountable for our financial responsibilities.

Peer Pressure and Lifestyle Inflation

Peer pressure and lifestyle inflation can also hinder our financial success. Many people feel the pressure to keep up with their peers or societal expectations, leading to overspending, lifestyle inflation, and financial strain.

Debunking the myth that we need to conform to societal norms or expectations involves understanding our own values, priorities, and financial goals. It also involves learning to say no to peer pressure, being mindful of our spending habits, and living within our means, regardless of external influences.

In conclusion, overcoming psychological barriers to financial success involves cultivating a positive money mindset, managing emotional spending, addressing fears of failure or success, overcoming procrastination and decision paralysis, and resisting peer pressure and lifestyle inflation. By addressing these psychological barriers, we can develop healthy financial habits and mindset that support our long-term financial success.

Conclusion: Embracing Financial Clarity and Empowerment

Throughout this book, we have challenged common money myths and debunked misconceptions about personal finance. We have explored practical strategies for managing money, debunked the myth of "get rich quick" schemes, discussed the importance of budgeting, saving, investing, and managing debt. We have also delved into the psychological barriers that can hinder our financial success, such as negative money mindsets, emotional spending, fear of failure or success, procrastination, and peer pressure.

By challenging the status quo and debunking these money myths, we have gained a deeper understanding of how to effectively manage our finances and create a path to financial success. We have learned that financial success is not just about accumulating wealth, but also about developing a healthy relationship with money, aligning our spending with our values and priorities, and overcoming psychological barriers that can impede our progress.

As we conclude this book, it's important to reflect on the key lessons learned and embrace financial clarity and empowerment. Here are some key takeaways:

- Financial education is essential: Understanding basic financial concepts, developing budgeting and saving habits, and learning how to invest and manage debt are crucial for achieving long-term financial success. It's important to continue learning and educating ourselves about personal finance to make informed financial decisions.

- Mindset matters: Our mindset and beliefs about money play a significant role in our financial behaviors and outcomes. Cultivating a positive money mindset based on abundance, gratitude, and empowerment can help us make better financial decisions and overcome psychological barriers to financial success.

- Emotions impact finances: Emotions, such as stress, boredom, or peer pressure, can impact our financial behaviors, leading to impulsive spending, overspending, or lifestyle inflation. Developing healthy coping mechanisms for dealing with emotions and being mindful of our emotional triggers can help us avoid emotional spending and make more rational financial decisions.

- Proactivity is key: Taking proactive steps, such as budgeting, saving, investing, and managing debt, is crucial for achieving financial success. Avoiding procrastination, making timely financial decisions, and holding ourselves accountable for our financial responsibilities are key to building a strong financial foundation.

- Personal values guide spending: Aligning our spending with our personal values and priorities can help us make intentional financial decisions that support our long-term financial goals. Avoiding lifestyle inflation and peer pressure, and living within our means, can prevent us from overspending and accumulating unnecessary debt.

In conclusion, by challenging money myths, embracing financial education, developing a positive money mindset, managing emotions, being proactive, and aligning spending with personal values, we can overcome psychological barriers and achieve financial clarity and empowerment. Remember, financial success is a journey, and it's never too late to start taking positive steps towards a more secure financial future. Let's embrace financial clarity and empowerment and take control of our financial destinies!

Epilogue: Rewriting Your Money Story for a Brighter Financial Future

Congratulations! You have reached the end of this book, and hopefully, you have gained valuable insights and strategies for managing your money and achieving financial success. As you reflect on the journey you have taken throughout these pages, it's time to consider how you can rewrite your money story for a brighter financial future.

Your money story is the narrative you have created around money based on your upbringing, experiences, beliefs, and behaviors. It's shaped by external factors such as societal norms, cultural influences, and personal circumstances. However, you have the power to rewrite your money story and shape your financial future.

Now that you have gained a deeper understanding of personal finance, it's time to take action and make intentional changes in your financial behaviors. Here are some steps you can take to rewrite your money story for a brighter financial future:

Set clear financial goals: Define your short-term, medium-term, and long-term financial goals. Make them specific, measurable, achievable, relevant, and time-bound (SMART). Setting clear goals gives you a sense of direction and motivates you to take action towards achieving them.

Create a realistic budget: Based on your financial goals, create a budget that aligns your income with your expenses. Track your spending, identify areas where you can cut back, and prioritize saving and investing. Regularly review and adjust your budget as needed.

Build an emergency fund: Start building an emergency fund to provide a financial safety net for unexpected expenses. Aim to save three to six months' worth of living expenses in a separate savings account that is easily accessible.

Invest wisely: Learn about different investment options, such as stocks, bonds, real estate, and retirement accounts, and create a diversified investment portfolio that aligns with your risk tolerance and financial goals. Seek professional advice if needed.

Manage debt strategically: If you have debt, develop a plan to pay it off strategically. Prioritize high-interest debts, such as credit card debt, and consider consolidating or refinancing debts to lower interest rates and reduce monthly payments.

Cultivate a positive money mindset: Reflect on your beliefs and attitudes about money, and consciously cultivate a positive money mindset based on abundance, gratitude, and empowerment. Practice self-awareness and challenge negative money beliefs that may be holding you back.

Be mindful of emotions: Be aware of how emotions can impact your financial decisions, and practice mindfulness when it comes to spending and investing. Avoid impulsive spending or making financial decisions based solely on emotions.

Seek continuous financial education: Keep learning and improving your financial literacy. Stay updated with the latest personal finance trends, strategies, and tools. Attend workshops, read books, follow reputable financial blogs, and seek advice from trusted financial professionals.

Remember, rewriting your money story takes time and effort. It's a journey that requires consistent commitment, discipline, and self-reflection. But with determination and the right strategies in place, you can create a brighter financial future for yourself and your loved ones.

As you embark on this new chapter of your financial journey, remember to stay focused on your goals, be proactive in managing your money, and stay true to your values. Embrace financial clarity and empowerment, and let your new money story be one of financial success, abundance, and peace of mind. Here's to a brighter financial future for you!

Appendix: Tools and Resources for Financial Literacy

In today's complex financial landscape, it's crucial to have access to reliable tools and resources that can help you navigate the world of personal finance. The following are some recommendations for tools and resources that can enhance your financial literacy and empower you to make informed financial decisions.

- Personal Finance Apps: There are numerous personal finance apps available for smartphones and tablets that can help you track your expenses, create budgets, and manage your investments. Popular apps include Mint, Personal Capital, and You Need a Budget (YNAB), among others.

- Online Budgeting Tools: Many websites offer free online budgeting tools that allow you to create and track your budget. These tools often provide visualizations of your spending habits, savings goals, and debt management progress. Examples include BudgetTracker, EveryDollar, and Budgetpulse.

- Financial News Websites: Stay informed about the latest news and trends in personal finance by following reputable financial news websites. Websites like CNBC, Bloomberg, and Reuters provide up-to-date information on markets, investing, and personal finance topics.

- Government Websites: Many government agencies offer valuable resources for financial literacy. For example, the U.S. government's official website, USA.gov, provides information on various financial topics, including taxes, Social Security, and consumer protection.

- Financial Education Websites: There are numerous websites dedicated to providing financial education and resources. Websites like Investopedia, The Balance, and Financial Literacy and Education Commission offer a wealth of information on personal finance, investing, and retirement planning.

- Books on Personal Finance: There are countless books available on personal finance that cover a wide range of topics, from budgeting and investing to debt management and retirement planning. Some popular titles include "Rich Dad Poor Dad" by Robert Kiyosaki, "The Total Money Makeover" by Dave Ramsey, and "Your Money or Your Life" by Vicki Robin.

- Financial Literacy Programs: Many organizations and non-profits offer financial literacy programs and workshops. These programs provide education and resources on topics such as budgeting, saving, investing, and debt management. Examples include the National Endowment for Financial Education (NEFE), Financial Peace University by Dave Ramsey, and the Money Smart program by the Federal Deposit Insurance Corporation (FDIC).

- Financial Advisors: If you feel overwhelmed or need personalized guidance, consider seeking help from a certified financial advisor. A financial advisor can provide tailored advice on budgeting, investing, retirement planning, and other financial matters based on your individual circumstances and goals.

- Online Courses: There are numerous online courses available that focus on various aspects of personal finance. These courses often provide structured lessons, quizzes, and practical exercises to enhance your financial knowledge and skills. Platforms like Coursera, Udemy, and LinkedIn

Learning offer a wide range of personal finance courses taught by industry experts.

By utilizing these tools and resources, you can improve your financial literacy and make informed financial decisions. Remember to verify the credibility and reliability of the sources you use and always do your due diligence before making any financial decisions. Financial literacy is an ongoing journey, so continue to educate yourself and empower yourself with knowledge to achieve your financial goals.

www.ingramcontent.com/pod-product-compliance
Lightning Source LLC
Chambersburg PA
CBHW071144220526
45467CB00015B/1886